CW00328175

THE RESOURCE FOR SMALL GROUP WORSHIP

VOLUME ONE

Devised by Chris Bowater

Kevin Mayhew

First published in 2000 by
KEVIN MAYHEW LTD
Buxhall
Stowmarket
Suffolk IP14 3BW

© 2000 Chris Bowater

The right of Chris Bowater to be identified as the author and compiler
of this work has been asserted by him in accordance with
the Copyright Designs and Patents Act 1988.

The Worship Sessions in this book (excluding the words and music of the songs)
may be photocopied provided they are used for the purpose for which the
book is intended. Reproduction of any of the contents of this book for
commercial purposes is subject to the usual copyright restrictions.
Please see next page for details regarding song copyright.

No other part of this publication may be reproduced, stored in
a retrieval system, or transmitted, in any form or by any means,
electronic, mechanical, photocopying or otherwise, without
the prior written permission of the publisher.

All rights reserved.

ISBN 184003 510 2
ISMN M57004 667 6
Catalogue No. 1450170

Illustrations by E Margaret Inkpen
Cover design by Jonathan Stroulger
Edited by Helen Elliot
Project Co-ordinator: Asher Gregory

Printed in Great Britain

Important Copyright Information Regarding the Songs in this Book

The Publishers wish to express their gratitude to the copyright owners who have granted permission to include copyright material in this book. Details are indicated on the respective pages and on the acknowledgements page.

The **words** of the songs in this publication are covered by a **Church Copyright Licence** which allows local church reproduction on overhead projector acetates, in service bulletins, songsheets, audio/visual recording and other formats.

The **music** in this book is covered by the 'add-on' **Music Reproduction Licence** issued by CCL (Europe) Ltd and you may photocopy the music and words of the songs in this book provided:

- You hold a current Music Reproduction Licence from CCL (Europe) Ltd.
- The copyright owner of the hymn or song you intend to photocopy is included in the Authorised Catalogue List which comes with your Music Reproduction Licence.

Full details of both the Church Copyright Licence and the additional Music Reproduction Licence are available from:

Christian Copyright Licensing (Europe) Ltd
PO Box 1339
Eastbourne
East Sussex
BN21 1AD

Tel: 01323 417711
Fax: 01323 417722
e-mail: info@ccli.co.uk
WEB: www.ccli.com

Please note, all texts and music in this book are protected by copyright and if you do *not* possess a licence from CCL (Europe) Ltd, they may *not* be reproduced in any way for sale or private use without the consent of the copyright owner.

Creative Team

Devised by Chris Bowater

Editorial	E. Margaret Inkpen & Carol Woodcock
Writers	Jane Amey, E. Margaret Inkpen, Jo Pimlott, Pat Turner
Illustrations	E. Margaret Inkpen
Audio	Laurie Blackler & Daniel Bowater

Recorded at dB Studios, Lincoln

The Resource for Small Group Worship has been devised with convenience, variety and flexibility in mind. Taking into account also the breadth of worship experience and expression, this resource seeks to provide creative opportunities for 'all-age worship' without being either too condescending or too academic.

Contents

How to Use
The Resource for Small Group Worship

Convenience   For the all-too-busy group leader, this resource provides a complete worship experience that includes:

- Worship songs: gently contemporary, easy to follow without being predictable.
- Meditation: wordless worship, a time to pause, reflect, consider and listen to God.
- Bible readings: arranged for corporate, responsive or personal reading.
- Prayers: written in non-religious language, for corporate or personal use.
- Discussion topics: touching issues of faith, essentials of life, challenges in society.
- Creative activities: always fun, never too exclusive, certain to build group relationships.

Each worship session comes in two parts:

1 The Notes for Leader preparation section, which comprises:

   – an introduction to the theme
   – a list of resources required
   – notes for leading the session, with extracts from
   – relevant books and materials for further activities.

2 Worship Session material. The following icons are used to identify section of the worship material or format. *Only pages with a large underlying icon may be photocopied, or pages of artwork to be used by the group*:

 aOpening words (including worship song)

 Meditation and listening to God

 Reading from the Bible

 Prayer and praise (including worship songs)

Further activities, discussion, study and creative ideas

 Closing words

A full programme would take about 1 hour to complete.

Variety In order to provide as wide a range of material as possible, each volume of *The Resource for Small Group Worship* contains:

- three sessions of general worship
- one session aimed at families and children
- one session which focuses on social awareness and specific issues.

Flexibility *The Resource for Small Group Worship* can be used more selectively by leaders looking for:

- song selection
- meditation ideas
- thematic material
- specialist topics – e.g. social awareness, church festivals, seasonal issues, special occasions
- group activities – drama, craft-work and suchlike
- written prayers.

Though much of the groundwork has been done here for the group leader, the role of that leader is still crucial. Enlist the help of the Holy Spirit at all times so that the worship is truly 'in Spirit and truth'. Lead the people into an experience that more than fills a programme but also affects their homes, marriages, relationships, attitudes, and jobs: their whole lives.

May this resource be a blessing to you, your groups and churches.

Chris Bowater

SESSION 1

Notes for Leader

Session 1: General Worship

THEME: GOD, THE FATHER

Introduction to theme

Young people today are searching for true male identity and fatherhood qualities in parents. They often reject God as Father because of experiences in their family life. This session seeks to discover the real qualities of perfect fatherhood (or strictly speaking, parenthood, as God possesses characteristics of both male and female). God is our 'example'. Not only are we worshipping an almighty, majestic God, but also one we can call 'Abba, Father'.

With minimal preparation your group can use the optional dramatic readings of the 'Prodigal Son'. Try them!

Resources required

You will need enough copies of the session material for your group.

Worship songs:

These will be found on Album 1, tracks 1-4.

 Give thanks by Henry Smith

 Abba, Father by Dave Bilbrough

 O Father of the fatherless by Graham Kendrick

 Meditation track – *Journey*

Extract from *The Father Heart of God* by Floyd McClung, published by Kingsway Publications, Eastbourne, 1985.

 Optional – drama (see page 14), copy of passage (a), a reader, a father and son or 'Reading with a difference' (see page 14), copies of passage (b), 2 readers.

 Optional dramatic readings – Luke 15:11-20

Preparation

 Meditation and listening to God

Introduce the meditation by saying: Let us consider the Father heart of God. Jesus describes the Father's heart in the story of the 'Prodigal Son'.

- The Father loved his son so much that he let him leave home.

- The Father loved his son so deeply that he watched every day for his return.

- He loved his son so much that he did not condemn him, but forgave him and celebrated his return with a party!

Then read this passage:

'Despite all that the Bible teaches about God as loving and just, there was a time in my life when I respected him, but did not love him. I even feared him because of his awesome power, but I did not love him for his goodness. It was when I looked beyond my ideas about God, beyond my desires to argue and discuss and asked God to reveal how he saw my selfishness, that I began to experience a deeper relationship with a Father whose heart is broken because of us.'

Suggested time for meditation: 3-5 minutes

At the close of the meditation time:

Leader Jesus said, 'No one comes to the Father except through me. Anyone who has seen me has seen the Father.'

After closing the meditation, allow time for the group to share thoughts arising from the meditation time.

 Prayer and praise

Members of the group can use the prayers given or offer spontaneous prayers. The prayers can be cut up into individual prayers and placed centrally, or allocated to the members of the group.

 Further activities

The Bible references and material are based on Floyd McClung's book *The Father Heart of God*. Each prayer provided in the 'prayer and praise' section was based on a passage of scripture revealing God's qualities or characteristics (see 'References' page 26). In twos or threes suggest the group match the prayers and the passages. Explain these are the qualities we should be looking for and encouraging in parents today. Although we use the word 'Father' for God, we know that he possesses all the qualities of father and mother, showing his unique character. It is God's qualities that we look for in earthly parents, not the other way round. We cannot base our conception of God on the failings of human fathers.

Read this quote from *The Father Heart of God*:

One of the most wonderful revelations in the Bible is that God is our Father. However, every person seems to have a different idea of what God is like, because they unconsciously tend to attach feelings and impressions that they have of their own earthly father and other authority figures, to their concept of their heavenly Father. Good experiences bring us closer to knowing and understanding God, just as bad experiences create distorted pictures of the Father's love for us.

 Optional activities

(a) Drama with minimal preparation required, based on the reading of the 'Prodigal Son'.

A father from your group will be required to stand at the front of the group (this has more impact in a larger space) looking around the room and towards the back, waiting. A child, preferably his own son, aged between 6-10 years old, waits at the back of the group, or room.

A member of the group reads the parable in Luke 15:11-20.

The father looks up as if he has seen his son and can't believe it.

The child shouts, 'Daddy, I'm coming to you. Catch me!'

He runs to his father who catches him, hugs him, and swings him round.

The reader completes the reading, verses 21-24.

(b) Reading with a difference.

Using the familiar words of the parable, Luke 15:11-20, a reader continues with the following 'revised version':

But while he was still a long way off, his father saw him, and was filled with anger that his son would dare to come home after what he had done. He ran to meet him, shouting, 'Don't come back here, thinking you will be accepted back into the family. You chose to go your own way. Now, get out of here. I never want to see you again. You are no longer any son of mine.'

A member of the group shouts out, 'But that's not right. It's not what the Bible says.'

Reader continues:

No, it says that the Father ran to meet him and threw his arms around him and kissed him. He forgave his son everything, saying, 'My son was dead and is alive again, was lost and is found.' The household was called to celebrate. But that's not what would really happen, is it? I mean, the father just wouldn't react like that. It's all wrong.

Leader   No, it's us that have got it wrong. This is the way Father God would react. He loves us so much and is always waiting to forgive us with mercy and compassion.

 Closing words

Close the meeting by saying:

For so many people, the father they have experienced has fallen short of these qualities. God's fatherhood is perfect. Many people respond to God as a father by rejecting Him because of their own experience of an earthly father who did not love, was not kind, faithful or merciful, wise or strong.

But what would happen if we went to the seaside for the first time and found the beach dirty and littered with empty cans, bottles and plastic bags, the sea muddy and cold, the weather miserable? Our seaside experience a shattering failure? Do we say 'never again'? Or do we study the holiday brochures, listen to the stories of friends who have found 'the perfect beach' and go to make our own discovery? Not every seaside resort is a disappointment. If we really want to find that perfect beach we will search for it, and one day we will find it. So it must be with Father God.

It is suggested that one of the worship songs be used at the close of the meeting.

Worship Session 1

THEME: GOD, THE FATHER

Opening words

Leader I will proclaim the name of the Lord, Oh, praise the greatness of our God! He is the Rock, his works are perfect, and all his ways are just. A faithful God who does no wrong, upright and just is he.

(Deuteronomy 32:3-4)

Group *He is our Father, the Creator who made us and formed us. To him we cry, 'Abba, Father'.*

Leader The Lord is compassionate and gracious, slow to anger, abounding in love. As a father has compassion on his children, so the Lord has compassion on those who fear him.

(Psalm 103:8, 13)

Group *He is our Father, the Creator who made us and formed us. To him we cry, 'Abba, Father'.*

Worship song

Give thanks
Henry Smith

Give thanks with a grateful heart.
Give thanks to the Holy One.
Give thanks because he's given
Jesus Christ, his Son.
Give thanks with a grateful heart.
Give thanks to the Holy One.
Give thanks because he's given
Jesus Christ, his Son.

And now let the weak say, 'I am strong',
let the poor say, 'I am rich',
because of what the Lord has done for us.
And now let the weak say, 'I am strong',
let the poor say, 'I am rich',
because of what the Lord has done for us.
(Give thanks) *Last time*.

© 1978 Integrity's Hosanna! Music/Kingsway's Thankyou Music

Reading from the Psalms

Leader I will sing of the Lord's great love for ever; with my mouth I will make your faithfulness known through all generations.

Group *I will declare that your love stands firm for ever, that you established your faithfulness in heaven itself.*

Leader You said, 'I have made a covenant with my chosen one, I have sworn to David, my servant, I will establish your line for ever and make your throne firm through all generations.'

Group *The heavens praise your wonders, O Lord, your faithfulness in the great assembly. For who in the skies above can compare with the Lord? He is more awesome than any around Him.*

Leader O Lord God Almighty, who is like you? You are mighty, O Lord, and faithfulness surrounds you. The heavens are yours, and yours also the earth; you founded the world and all that is in it.

Group *Righteousness and justice are the foundation of your throne; love and faithfulness go before you.*

Leader Blessed are those who have learned to acclaim you, who walk in the light of Your presence, O Lord.

Group *They rejoice in your name all day long; for you are their glory and their strength.*

Leader You said, 'I have found a young man among the people, I have found David my servant. My hand will sustain him, surely my arm will strengthen him. My faithful love will be with him.'

Group *'He will call out to me, "You are my Father, my God, the Rock, my Saviour". I will maintain my love to him forever and my covenant with him will never fail.*

Leader 'I will establish his line forever, his throne as long as the heavens endure. I will not take my love from him, nor will I ever betray my faithfulness. I will not alter what my lips have uttered, even though his sons forsake my laws.'

Group *'Once for all, I have sworn by my holiness, and I will not lie. I will maintain my love to him for ever and my covenant with him will never fail.'*

Leader You are my Father, my God, the Rock my Saviour.

Group *To him we cry, 'Abba, Father'.*

Adapted from Psalm 89.

Meditation and listening to God

The following passage presents three aspects of the Father, based on the words from *The Father Heart of God* by Floyd McClung.

- The Father loved his son so much that he let him leave home.
- The Father loved his son so deeply that he watched every day for his return.
- He loved his son so much that he did not condemn him, but forgave him and celebrated his return with a party!

'Despite all that the Bible teaches about God as loving and just, there was a time in my life when I respected him, but did not love him. I even feared him because of his awesome power, but I did not love him for his goodness. It was when I looked beyond my ideas about God, beyond my desires to argue and discuss and asked God to reveal how he saw my selfishness, that I began to experience a deeper relationship with a Father whose heart is broken because of us.'

At the close of the meditation time:

Leader Jesus said, 'No one comes to the Father except through me. Anyone who has seen me has seen the Father.'

Prayer and praise

Father, thank you for creating us in your own image,
with freedom to choose our response to your love.
We are the work of your hands.

Amen.

Thank you, Father,
for providing for our physical, emotional, mental
and spiritual needs.
We only have to ask you, and seek your Kingdom.

Amen.

Your name is Wonderful Counsellor, Mighty God,
Everlasting Father, and Prince of Peace.
Thank you for leading and guiding us
in your wisdom and truth.

Amen.

Lord, you discipline those you love.
Thank you for being a father who loves us so much
that you correct us when we go wrong.

Amen.

Father, thank you for seeing something good
in our failures and weaknesses;
for searching for us when we are lost
and forgiving our faults.

Amen.

Thank you, Father, for being our strength and comfort in times of need.

Amen.

You are my refuge, my fortress,
my God in whom I trust.
You protect, defend and deliver your children.
We can rest in the shadow of your wing,
in the shelter of the Most High.
Thank you, Father.

Amen.

Thank you for revealing yourself to us through your Son, Jesus.
Thank you for loving us so much that you sent your Son to reconcile us to you.

Amen.

Worship songs

Abba, Father
Dave Bilbrough

Abba, Father, let me be
yours and yours alone.
May my will forever be
more and more your own.

Never let my heart grow cold,
never let me go.
Abba, Father, let me be
yours and yours alone.

© 1977 Kingsway's Thankyou Music

O Father of the fatherless
Graham Kendrick

O Father of the fatherless
in whom all families are blessed,
I love the way you father me.
You gave me life, forgave the past,
now in your arms I'm safe at last;
I love the way you father me.

Continued over

Father me, for ever you'll father me,
and in your embrace
I'll be for ever secure;
I love the way you father me. (repeat)

When bruised and broken I draw near
you hold me close and dry my tears;
I love the way you father me.
At last my fearful heart is still,
surrendered to your perfect will;
I love the way you father me.

If in my foolishness I stray,
returning empty and ashamed,
I love the way you father me.
Exchanging for my wretchedness
your radiant robes of righteousness,
I love the way you father me.

And when I look into your eyes,
from deep within my spirit cries,
I love the way you father me.
Before such love I stand amazed
and ever will through endless days;
I love the way you father me.

© 1992 Make Way Music

Prayer may continue as appropriate.

Further activities   The following references are based on Floyd McClung's book *The Father Heart of God*. Each prayer provided in the 'prayer and praise' section is based on a passage of scripture revealing God's qualities or characteristics as listed below.

References:

1   Father accepts us as we are. He made us.
Isaiah 64:8.

2   Father knows our needs and cares about our daily lives.
Matthew 6:25-32; Matthew 7:11; Psalm 52:22.

3   Father disciplines in love.
Hebrews 12:11; Psalm 94:12; Revelation 3:19.

4   Father is patient and shows mercy and forgiveness.
Psalm 103:8, 12-13; Psalm 78:35-39; Nehemiah 9:17-19.

5   Father comforts us.
2 Corinthians 1:3.

6   Father protects and defends us.
Psalm 91:1-3.

7   Father cares for the vulnerable.
Psalm 68:5-6.

8   Father loves his children.
2 Corinthians 6:18; John 16:27.

9   Father is wise and strong, faithful and just.
1 Corinthians 1:25; Isaiah 40:28-29; Deuteronomy 32:4.

10   Father is powerful but gentle.
1 Kings 19:12; Isaiah 40:25-26.

These are the qualities we should be looking for and encouraging in parents today. Although we use the word 'Father' for God, we know that he possesses all the qualities of father and mother, showing his unique character. It is God's qualities that we look for in earthly parents, not the other way round. We cannot base our conception of God on the failings of human fathers.

Closing words For so many people, the father they have experienced has fallen short of these qualities. God's fatherhood is perfect. Many people respond to God as a father by rejecting him because of their own experience of an earthly father who did not love, was not kind, faithful or merciful, wise or strong.

But what would happen if we went to the seaside for the first time and found the beach dirty and littered with empty cans, bottles and plastic bags, the sea muddy and cold, the weather miserable? Our seaside experience a shattering failure? Do we say 'never again'? Or do we study the holiday brochures, listen to the stories of friends who have found 'the perfect beach' and go to make our own discovery? Not every seaside resort is a disappointment. If we really want to find that perfect beach we will search for it, and one day we will find it. So it must be with Father God.

Give thanks with a grateful heart

Words and Music: Henry Smith

© Copyright 1978 Integrity's Hosanna! Music. Administered by Kingsway's
Thankyou Music, P.O. Box 75, Eastbourne, East Sussex, BN23 6NW, UK. (For the UK only.) Used by permission.

Abba, Father, let me be

Words and Music: Dave Bilbrough arr. Christopher Tambling

© Copyright 1977 Kingsway's Thankyou Music, P.O. Box 75, Eastbourne,
East Sussex, BN23 6NW, UK. Used by permission.

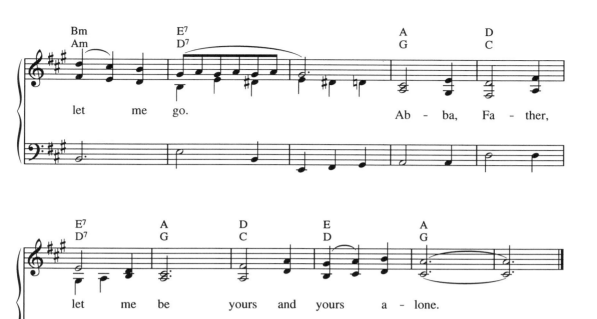

let me go.   Ab - ba, Fa - ther,

let me be   yours and   yours a - lone.

O Father of the fatherless
Father me

Words and Music: Graham Kendrick

© Copyright 1992 Make Way Music, P.O. Box 263, Croydon, Surrey, CR9 5AP, UK.
International copyright secured. All rights reserved. Used by permission.

2. When bruised and broken I draw near,
   you hold me close and dry my tears;
   I love the way you father me.
   At last my fearful heart is still,
   surrendered to your perfect will;
   I love the way you father me.

3. If in my foolishness I stray,
   returning empty and ashamed,
   I love the way you father me.
   Exchanging for my wretchedness
   your radiant robes of righteousness,
   I love the way you father me.

4. And when I look into your eyes,
   from deep within my spirit cries,
   I love the way you father me.
   Before such love I stand amazed
   and ever will through endless days;
   I love the way you father me.

SESSION 2

Notes for Leader

Session 2: General Worship

THEME: LOVE

Introduction to theme

Love is quite an overwhelming subject and could be presented in many ways. This session touches on three aspects of love – God's love for us, our love for God and love for others. It also looks at love as 'the fulfilment of God's law' (Romans 13:10). This may sound rather legalistic, but it can also be life changing! Many people question a God of love who allows evil and tragedy in His world. We need to see what the Bible teaches about God's love and our responsibility towards others.

Each person in the group should leave the meeting having experienced a new touch from God and a sense of caring within the group, as well as reaching out in love.

Resources required

You will need enough copies of the session material for your group.

Worship songs:

These will be found on Album 1, tracks 5-8.

 *When I feel the touch* by Keri Jones and David Matthew

Ⓟ *Overwhelmed by love* by Noel Richards

Ⓟ *Here is love* by William Rees and Robert Lowry

Ⓜ Meditation track – *Reflection*

1 Corinthians 13:4-7, from *The Living Bible*, published by Tyndale House, Wheaton, Illinois, USA 1971.

 Extracts from *Balcony People* by Joyce Landorf, published by Word Books, Waco, Texas, USA. 1984.

 Optional activity

- red heart shapes cut out of construction paper or card (see page 42)
- red or white ribbon
- glue and pens.

 Extracts from *Rooted in God* by Marcia Hollis, published by The Anglican Book Centre, Toronto, Canada.

Preparation

 Reading from Scripture

The first reading can be taken alternately, leader and group. Ask each member of the group to read a line in turn of paraphrased passage from 1 Corinthians 13:4-7.

 Meditation and listening to God

Introducing the thought for meditation:

In our time of silence we are going to think how we express our love for others and how we have been blessed by those who love us. Let me read a short passage from Joyce Landorf's book *Balcony People*. She describes 'basement people' as those who pull us down and 'balcony people' as those who lift us up and inspire us.

This is how she describes them:

Think of it! All around that sphere of clear air in our conscious minds, runs a balcony filled with people who are not merely sitting there, but practically hanging over the rails, cheering us on! There was my mother, who always told me I was special, leaning over the rail smiling. I could see my family and a small but beautiful group of friends. The Lord was there and Paul, David and Peter. Then I thought of the names of people to whom I was a 'balcony person'.

Joyce continues –

Balcony people love from the heart.
Balcony people listen from the heart.
Balcony people care from the heart.

To close:

Leader Be patient with each other, making allowances for each other's faults because of your love (Ephesians 4:2).

After the period of meditation, a few minutes could be spent in writing down, individually, the people who could be listed as 'balcony people' for each member of the group and also those to whom each person has been a 'balcony supporter'.

Suggested time for meditation: 3-5 minutes.

Before moving on, allow time for the group to share thoughts arising from the time of meditation.

 Further activity

There are a variety of ways of using the material for this part of the session. Suggested opening and closing paragraphs are given, or you may choose to use the references for discussion alone. Alternatively, do the activity and discuss the verses at the same time. You may wish people to look up the references in the Bible rather than make copies of the verses. Whichever way you spend this time, let it reflect these three aspects of love:

- God's love for us
- our love of God
- our love for others.

The Ten Commandments (Exodus 20:1–17) make a useful framework for discussing our love of God (Exodus 20:3, 6, 10–11) and our love for others (Exodus 20:12–17). The commandments are the 'Law of Love'. Discuss this topic, knowing that many people ask how, if God is a loving God, he can allow things like war, starvation, torture, disease, personal tragedy to happen. What can we learn about God's love? Is it conditional or unconditional? A list of verses is given which can be used for discussion, or for creative activity.

Creative activity option: each member of the group draws another person's name from a pile. Using the red heart-shaped cards (see page 40 for template), each person chooses a verse about God's love to write on the card. They can present their 'love card', reading the verse aloud and some may wish to pray with the recipient. The ribbon can be used for decoration, or a hanging loop. This activity can be a time of special blessing to those people who are not sure of God's love for them, or find it hard to accept his love.

 Closing words

Read this extract from *Rooted in God* by Marcia Hollis:

A good root system is the most important part of a plant. Nothing can survive for long without adequate roots. A tree or shrub with a good root system may be broken or cut back almost to the earth and still be able to regenerate itself. Similar damage to the root system will kill the tree.

Writing to the Ephesians, Paul prayed that they might have their roots and foundations in love and by this he meant the love of God. We should be rooted in God, who is the ground of our being. Roots have essentially two purposes in the life of a plant. The first is to nourish it, the second is to hold it up. Roots get nourishment from soil or ground. Plants have seasons of dryness. It is in these dry seasons that a plant extends its roots and pushes them down into the earth to search for water.

Similarly a tree that has been exposed to the tearing and pulling of the wind from its early days has had to send down roots deep enough to hold it in place.

St Augustine of Hippo wrote:

In the land of the living we ought to have a root. Let our root be there. That root is out of sight, its fruits may be seen, the root cannot be seen. Our root is our love; our fruits are our works. It is needful that thy works proceed from love; then is thy root in the land of the living.

It may be practical to suggest that the group stand in a circle, holding hands. Then pray:

I pray that you, being rooted and established in love, may have power, together with all the saints, to grasp how wide and long and high and deep is the love of Christ, and to know this love that surpasses knowledge – that you may be filled to the measure of all the fullness of God. Amen.

(Ephesians 3:17-19)

'Love Card' Template

this is my prayer
that your love may
abound
            more
            and
            more
    Phil. 1v.
        9-10

I pray that you
may know this
love that
surpasses
knowledge
Eph. 3 v. 19

Worship Session 2

THEME: LOVE

Opening words

Leader Love the Lord your God with all your heart and with all your soul and with all your strength. This is the first and greatest commandment. The second is similar: love your neighbour as yourself.

Love is the fulfilment of the law of God (Romans 13:10).

Group *Lord, fill me with love.*

Leader Behold what manner of love the Father has given to us, that we should be called children of God (1 John 3:1).

The Lord's unfailing love surrounds those who trust in him (Psalm 32:10).

Group *Love never fails.*

Leader Love is the fulfilment of the law of God. If we love God, we will do whatever he tells us to do and he has told us from the beginning to love one another (2 John 6).

Group *Love never fails. Lord, fill me with love.*

Worship song

When I feel the touch
Keri Jones and David Matthew

When I feel the touch
of your hand upon my life,
it causes me to sing a song
that I love you, Lord.
So from deep within
my spirit singeth unto thee,
You are my King,
You are my God,
and I love you, Lord.

© 1978 Word's Spirit of Praise Music/Copycare

Reading from Scripture

Leader and group read alternate verses from 1 John 4:7-19.

Leader Dear friends, let us love one another, for love comes from God. Everyone who loves has been born of God and knows God.

Group *Whoever does not love, does not know God, because God is love.*

Leader This is how God showed his love among us: He sent his one and only Son into the world that we might live through him.

Group *This is love: not that we loved God, but that he loved us and sent his Son as an atoning sacrifice for our sins.*

Leader Dear friends, since God so loved us, we also ought to love one another. No one has ever seen God; but if we love each other, God lives in us and his love is made complete in us.

Group *We know that we live in him and he in us, because he has given us of his spirit.*

Leader We have seen and testify that the Father has sent his Son to be Saviour of the world.

Group *If anyone acknowledges that Jesus is the Son of God, God lives in him and he in God and so we know and rely on the love God has for us.*

Leader God is love. Whoever lives in love, lives in God and God in him.

Group *Love is made complete among us so that we will have confidence on the day of judgement, because in this world we are like him.*

Leader There is no fear in love. But perfect love drives out fear, because fear has to do with punishment. The one who fears is not made perfect in love.

Group *We love because he first loved us and he has given us this command: whoever loves God must also love his brother.*

Leader Love is the fulfilment of the law of God.

Group *Lord, fill me with love.*

Adapted from 1 John 4:7-19

1 Corinthians 13:4-7 from *The Living Bible.*

Love is patient.

Love is kind.

Love is never jealous or envious.

Love is not boastful or proud.

Love is not haughty or selfish, or rude.

Love does not demand its own way.

Love is not irritable or touchy.

Love never holds grudges and will hardly ever notice when others do things wrong.

Love is never glad about injustice, but rejoices when the truth wins out.

If you love someone you will be loyal, no matter what the cost.

Love always believes and expects the best in a friend.

Love will always stand its ground to defend someone.

Other things may come to an end, but love goes on for ever.

Leader Love never fails.

Group *Lord, fill us with love.*

Meditation and listening to God

Thought for meditation:

In our time of silence we are going to think how we express our love for others and how we have been blessed by those who love us, starting with a short passage from Joyce Landorf's book *Balcony People*. She describes 'basement people' as those who pull us down and 'balcony people' as those who lift us up and inspire us:

Think of it! All around that sphere of clear air in our conscious minds, runs a balcony filled with people who are not merely sitting there, but practically hanging over the rails, cheering us on! There was my mother, who always told me I was special, leaning over the rail smiling. I could see my family and a small but beautiful group of friends. The Lord was there and Paul, David and Peter. Then I thought of the names of people to whom I was a 'balcony person'.

Joyce continues –

Balcony people love from the heart.
Balcony people listen from the heart.
Balcony people care from the heart.

Let's take time to think of the people in our balcony and how we can be balcony people to others.

To close:

Leader Be patient with each other, making allowances for each other's faults because of your love (Ephesians 4:2).

Prayer and praise

Individual members of the group can read the following prayers. Others may prefer to use spontaneous prayers, offering their love to God and praying for others.

Love is patient.

Father, help me to be patient in difficult situations
and with people who irritate me.
Help me to wait for you
and be content with what I have at this moment.
Fill me with love for you and for others.
Thank you for loving me with such patience, Lord.

Amen.

Love is kind.

May my thoughts and actions be done in kindness, Lord.
Your loving kindness to me is more than life itself.
It is like arms gently wrapped around me
and sheltering me.
Help me to show kindness to those in desperate need
of love.

Amen.

Love does not envy.

I am constantly wishing I could be like other people,
envying their gifts; wanting what they have,
thinking I would be better off if I lived their lives.
Father, fill my heart with love
so that there is no room for greed and envy.

Amen.

Love does not boast.

Lord, forgive me for wanting other people
to think I am better than them,
for wanting to be No. 1.
I only want to be the best for you.
I will boast in you, Lord, and what you have done.
I will ask for no reward except your love.
It is your greatness and your power that are at work in
my life.

Amen.

Love is not proud.

Father, teach me humility;
teach me the meaning of meekness,
as Moses knew it,
single-minded in his walk with you, Lord.
I want to love you with my whole heart and soul
and strength.
I want to give my love to others, as you have loved me.

Amen.

Love is not self-seeking.

Your love, Lord God, was poured out for me.
Your Son gave His life for me.
I ask for nothing else but your love
and I give you my love.
Help me, Father, to pour out your love
into the lives of those around me, who need you so
much.

Amen.

Love keeps no record of wrongs.

Father, you have put the record of my sins
as far away as the East is from the West.

You keep no record of the things I have done against you.
Help me to forgive and forget
and stop harbouring grudges and resentment.
Lord, fill me with love.

Amen.

Love always protects.

Father, help me to love the needy and the vulnerable;
the weak and those with disabilities;
people who are at risk
from exploitation and discrimination.
To love and care from my heart, with your love.

Amen.

Love always trusts and hopes.

My hope is in you, my God, my Redeemer. I trust in you.
Father, help me to be one in whom others can trust;
let my love be trustworthy.

Amen.

Love always perseveres.

It is so easy, Father, to give up on love,
when you get nothing in return, or love is rejected.
Help me to understand, to care, to listen
and to keep loving.
You have persevered in your love for me
when I have turned away, Lord.
Thank you.

Amen.

Leader Love is the fulfilment of the law of God.

Group Love never fails. Lord, fill us with love.

Worship songs

Overwhelmed by love
Noel Richards

Overwhelmed by love

deeper than oceans,

high as the heavens.

Ever-living God,

your love has rescued me.

All my sin was laid

on your dear Son,

your precious One.

All my debt he paid,

great is your love for me

No one could ever earn your love

your grace and mercy is free.

Lord, these words are true,

so is my love for you.

© 1994 Kingsway's Thankyou Music

Here is love
William Rees

Here is love vast as the ocean,
loving kindness as the flood.
When the Prince of Life, our ransom,
shed for us his precious blood.
Who his love will not remember?
Who can cease to sing his praise?
He can never be forgotten
throughout heaven's eternal days.

On the mount of crucifixion
fountains opened deep and wide.
Through the floodgates of God's mercy
flowed a vast and gracious tide.
Grace and love, like mighty rivers,
poured incessant from above,
and heaven's peace and perfect justice
kissed a guilty world in love.

To close

Leader God so loved the world that he gave his one and only Son, that whosoever believes in him should not perish but have everlasting life (John 3:16).

Group *Lord, accept our love.*

Further activity

Leader 'Love is the fulfilment of the law,' says Paul in his letter to the Romans. What does the Bible teach us about God's law? Paul continues: 'Let no debt remain outstanding except the continuing debt to love one another, for he who loves his fellow man has fulfilled the law. The commandments are summed up in this one rule: "Love your neighbour as yourself." Love does no harm to its neighbour' (Romans 13:8-10).

Psalm 119 lays down the importance of following God's law, being obedient to the law, considering the law, living according to the law, being steadfast in the law, meditating on it, consumed with longing for it, setting one's heart on it, being taught by it. Remember – love is the fulfilment of the law and what do we gain from following God's law? The Bible says we are blessed by it, blameless, never put to shame, able to praise God with an upright heart, not forsaken, pure in heart, never sinning against God, no longer strangers, alive, having freedom of heart, finding delight, salvation and the Lord's unfailing love . . . and much, much more!

It is definitely worth studying the law – and love is its fulfilment! The Ten Commandments (Exodus 20:1-17) make a useful framework for discussing our love of

God (Exodus 20:3, 6, 10-11) and our love for others (Exodus 20:12-17). The commandments are the 'Law of Love'. Discuss this topic, knowing that many people ask how, if God is a loving God, he can allow things like war, starvation, torture, disease, personal tragedy to happen. What can we learn about God's love? Is it conditional or unconditional?

The following verses show the depth of God's love:

John 3:16.

God so loved the world that he gave His one and only Son that whoever believes in him shall not perish but have eternal life.

John 15:12-13.

My command is this: Love each other as I have loved you. Greater love has no one than this, that he lay down his life for his friends.

Romans 12:9-10

Love must be sincere. Hate what is evil; cling to what is good. Be devoted to one another in brotherly love. Honour one another above yourselves.

Philippians 1:9-10.

And this is my prayer: that your love may abound more and more in knowledge and depth of insight, so that you may be able to discern what is best and may be pure and blameless until the day of Christ.

2 Corinthians 2:4.

For I wrote to you out of great distress and anguish of heart and with many tears, not to grieve you, but to let you know the depth of my love for you.

John 11:33-36.

When Jesus saw her weeping, and the Jews who had come along with her also weeping, he was deeply moved in spirit and troubled. 'Where have you laid him?' he asked. 'Come and see, Lord,' they replied. Jesus wept. Then the Jews said, 'See how he loved him.'

Ephesians 3:17-19.

I pray that you, being rooted and established in love, may have power to grasp how wide and long and high and deep is the love of Christ, and to know this love that surpasses knowledge – that you may be filled to the measure of all the fullness of God.

Closing words

Writing to the Ephesians, Paul prayed that they might have their roots and foundations in love and by this he meant the love of God. We should be rooted in God, who is the ground of our being. Roots have essentially two purposes in the life of a plant. The first is to nourish it, the second is to hold it up. Roots get nourishment from soil or ground. Plants have seasons of dryness. It is in these dry seasons that a plant extends its roots and pushes them down into the earth to search for water.

Similarly a tree that has been exposed to the tearing and pulling of the wind from its early days has had to send down roots deep enough to hold it in place.

St Augustine of Hippo wrote:

In the land of the living we ought to have a root. Let our root be there. That root is out of sight, its fruits may be seen, the root cannot be seen. Our root is our love; our fruits are our works. It is needful that thy works proceed from love; then is thy root in the land of the living.

When I feel the touch

Words and Music: Keri Jones and David Matthew

© Copyright 1978 Word's Spirit of Praise Music. Administered by CopyCare,
P.O. Box 77, Hailsham, East Sussex, BN27 3EF, UK. (music@copycare.com) Used by permission.

Overwhelmed by love

Words and Music: Noel Richards

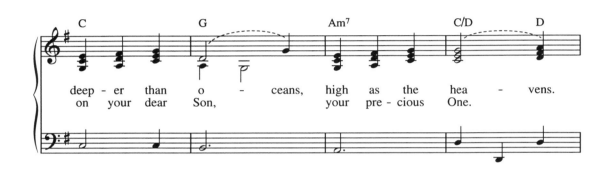

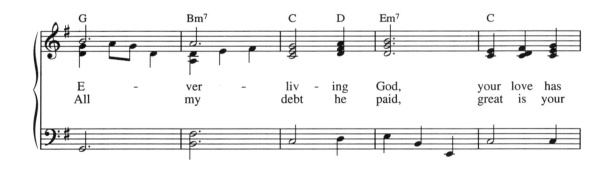

© Copyright 1994 Kingsway's Thankyou Music, P.O. Box 75, Eastbourne, East Sussex, BN23 6NW, UK. Used by permission.

Here is love

Words: William Rees
Music: Robert Lowry

DIM OND IESU

1. Here is love vast as the o - cean, lov - ing kind - ness as the flood. When the Prince of Life, our ran - som, shed for us his pre-cious blood. Who his love will not re - mem - ber? Who can cease to sing his praise? He can ne - ver be for - got - ten, through-out heav'n's e - ter - nal days.

2. On the mount of crucifixion
fountains opened deep and wide;
through the floodgates of God's mercy
flowed a vast and gracious tide.
Grace and love, like mighty rivers,
poured incessant from above,
and heaven's peace and perfect justice
kissed a guilty world in love.

SESSION 3

Notes for Leader

Session 3: General Worship

THEME: HOLINESS

Introduction to theme

The holiness of God leaves us standing in total awe, often creating a distance or separation between 'earthly me' and heavenly God. And yet he says that we are called to be holy too. Most people think a holy life too difficult to attain, and after all 'we are only human'! Holiness is beyond reach.

This session starts with worship, bringing us into a close relationship with a holy God, and leads us on to study and discussion which hopefully will make living to the glory of God more understandable and possible. It may require more than one session to work through the material, and hours of personal time with God to make an individual commitment to holiness – a life lived wholly for the Lord. The group will need to help each other in prayer and encouragement.

Resources required

You will need enough copies of the session material for your group, pens or pencils and Bibles.

Worship songs:

These will be found on Album 1, tracks 9-12:

 Only by grace by Gerrit Gustafson

 All to Jesus by J.W. Van De Venter

 Purify my heart by Brian Doerksen

 Meditation track – *Nearly in three-quarters*

A card with the word JAHWEH, a candle, a bowl of salt water.

  Extracts from *Let the Light Shine* by Derek Osborne, published by Falcon Booklets, CPAS Publications.

Preparation

 Meditation and listening to God

Read these extracts from *Let the Light Shine* by Derek Osborne:

Holiness of life is living to the glory of God.

Holiness can conjure up, rightly or wrongly, a picture of a predictable pattern of behaviour, a boring picture of do's and don'ts, which Christians must conform to.

It may suggest a sort of 'group character' and to be 'out of step' is to put a question mark on your own personal holiness.

We have been conditioned to think from the wrong end. Holiness must take its meaning from the 'glory of God'.

It is the product of indomitable, jealous, glad, reckless concern for God's glory.

I will find my highest personal holiness when I lose myself in a desire to extol the worth, reputation, honour and splendour of God the Father, God the Son and God the Holy Spirit.

Glory to God's holiness is what the Bible is all about. We need to get it into focus.

Repeat the italicised passage as a focus for meditation.

Suggested time for meditation: 3-5 minutes.

To close:

Leader You shall be holy unto me because I the Lord am holy.

Before moving on, allow time for the group to share any thoughts arising from the time of meditation.

 Further activity

The following material is based on three key words used by Derek Osborne in *Let the Light Shine*. It is suggested that each person in the group start with a copy of the page with headings and a pen or pencil. This gives an opportunity to make note of the references and go over the material at home.

The introductory section and paragraphs under each heading can be read to the group, or used as guidelines for the basis of discussion. Alternatively, the references alone can provide your material.

Suggestions for discussion:

1 Encourage the group to share their feelings of acceptance as an adopted child of God.

2 What do the group think of obligations/responsibilities of a 'holy life' based on the definition below?

3 Discuss 'being' and 'doing' – a swimmer is one who swims, a photographer takes photos, a painter paints – therefore a Christian ('being') does . . . what?

Introduce the subject, 'Living a Holy Life', using extracts from *Let the Light Shine* as follows:

Holiness of life is best defined in terms of living to the glory of God.

Acceptance, obligation and enablement are three key words which spell out the actual content of a holy life lived to the glory of God. All three concepts converge in Christ; our acceptance with the Father is in Christ; our obligation is to be like Christ and our enablement by the Holy Spirit is through Christ. Abiding in Christ is the central secret.

Without knowing God, we can hardly live to his glory. Without the Bible, we will make God in our own image. It is here that Jesus may be found and if the three key words are to have meaning and content, then it is from the scriptures that one can find the truth.

Acceptance

Our lives need to be dominated by the truth of the Father's adoption and its meaning:

- Adoption – no pretending – accepted in Christ – secure in the Father's love.
- No more insecurity or feeling inferior.
- No rejection of self, wanting to be different, longing to be like someone else.
- God made us, and redeemed us. He knows our sins, weaknesses, and disadvantages. Through his grace they can be turned to strengths and used for his purpose.
- Acceptance means trusting. God has accepted us in order that our faith shall not fail.
- Acceptance means dependence on the Father: He knows our needs, and how we feel. We cast our burdens on him.
- Acceptance through adoption leads to acceptance of our brothers and sisters in Christ – we are all his children and accepted into God's family.

We need to be sure of our own status as a child of God to learn about holiness of life.

Discuss these definitions.

References: Ephesians 1:4, 8; Romans 8:15-17; 2 Corinthians 6:18; Galatians 3:26-28; 4:6-7; Hebrews 12:7-8.

Obligation

'Living to the glory of Jesus Christ must mean demonstrating his truth as well as his grace. Such a life will obviously be characterised by veracity, integrity and identity.'

Our obligation as Christians is to live out holiness in grace and truth:

- Being honest and straightforward in speaking;
- open and natural, honest about our failures as part of our integrity;
- not thinking too highly of ourselves, nor being pseudo-humble.

By God's grace we can fulfil our potential. We need to live out the truths of the Gospel. God's promises are not empty words – they are trustworthy.

'Confusion, despair, apathy and inertia' are not living out the truth. Nor are 'living in a fantasy world or wishful thinking'. We need to face up to things without fear. There is 'strength in a greater reality – God'. We need to see things in their true perspective, not as 'gloomy imaginings of what might happen or dread of failure. Truth means shutting one's eyes to ugliness, injustice, error, and intrusions of sin.

Holiness shows a balance of grace and truth, as seen at Calvary. 'There we see the stark truth about sin as a terrible reality condemned by God, who must be true to his own essential holiness. There we see amazing grace which identifies with sinners and willingly endures the agonising experience of being abandoned by God and of dying in their place.

Being accepted in Christ, we have an obligation to live like Christ.

Discuss these definitions.

References: John 1:16-17; Acts 6:8; Ephesians 2:4-5; Colossians 4:6; Hebrews 12:14-15; Proverbs 22:11; 2 Corinthians 5:20-21, 6:3-10.

Enablement

'It is the glory of the Holy Spirit that enables the Christian to be and to do what God wants of him and to integrate these two things.' Holiness is the Holy Spirit in action in my life. 'Like learning to swim, we need to take our foot off the bottom! To prove the reality of God's truth in our lives, we need to swim in it!'

Discuss these definitions.

References: Galatians 5:16; Romans 7:15-23; Galatians 5:19-22; 2 Timothy 1:7; Philippians 4:13; 2 Timothy 1:6-7.

 ## Further activity (optional)

This activity could be fitted in before the discussion period. It allows a time to relax and chat, before study! Make copies of the verse over from 2 Corinthians 4:6. Cut into sections as shown. Make enough copies for your group to work in twos or threes. Allow two to three minutes to put the words in order to complete the verse. (Don't let the group know the reference before they start the activity!)

2 Corinthians 4:6.

FOR GOD WHO SAID	LET LIGHT SHINE
OUT OF DARKNESS	MADE HIS LIGHT SHINE
IN OUR HEARTS	TO GIVE US
THE LIGHT	OF THE KNOWLEDGE
OF THE GLORY	OF GOD
IN THE FACE	OF CHRIST

Worship Session 3

THEME: HOLINESS

Opening words

Leader (placing the card with JAHWEH written on it, on a central table)

In Old Testament time, the name of God was never spoken, but referred to with reverence as Jahweh, to sound like a breath. He was known as holy and awesome.

The Lord says: 'I will show my greatness and my holiness, and I will make my self known in the sight of many nations. Then they will know that I am the Lord'. *(Ezekiel 38:23)*

Group *Holy, holy, holy is the Lord.*

Leader You are to be holy to me, because I, the Lord, am holy and I have set you apart to be my own. *(Leviticus 20:26)*

Group *Holy, holy, holy is the Lord.*

Leader Let us purify ourselves from everything that contaminates body and spirit, perfecting holiness out of reverence for God. *(2 Corinthians 7:1)*

(The leader places the bowl of salt on a central table)

Leader Salt is a symbol of purity.

Group *We are the salt of the earth.*

(The leader lights the candle on the table)

Leader Light is a symbol of God's presence.

Group *Lord, let your light shine through us, so that we can be light to the world.*

Leader We have been set apart to be God's holy people.

Worship song

Only by grace
Gerrit Gustafsen

Only by grace can we enter,
only by grace can we stand;
not by our human endeavour,
but by the blood of the Lamb.
Into your presence you call us,
you call us to come.
Into your presence you draw us,
and now by your grace we come,
now by your grace we come.

Lord, if you marked our transgressions
who would stand?
Thanks to your grace we are cleansed
by the blood of the Lamb.
Lord, if you marked our transgressions
who would stand?
Thanks to your grace we are cleansed
by the blood of the Lamb.

© 1990 Integrity's Hosanna! Music/Kingsway's Thankyou Music

Reading from the Psalms

Leader Sing to the Lord a new song;
sing to the Lord, all the earth.
Sing to the Lord, praise his name,
proclaim his salvation day after day.

Group *Declare his glory among the nations,*
his marvellous deeds among all the people.
For great is the Lord and most worthy of praise.

Leader He is to be feared above all gods,
for all the gods of the nations are idols,
but the Lord made the heavens.

Group *Splendour and majesty are before him,*
strength and glory are in his sanctuary.

Leader Ascribe to the Lord, O families of nations,
ascribe to the Lord glory and strength.
Ascribe to the Lord the glory due his name;
bring an offering and come into his courts.

Group *Worship the Lord in the beauty of his holiness;*
bow down before him, all the earth.
Say among the nations, 'The Lord reigns'.

Leader The Lord reigns; let the nations tremble.

Group *Great is the Lord in Zion,*
he is exalted over all the nations.

Leader Let them praise your great and awesome name:
you are holy.

Group *Exalt the Lord our God and worship at his footstool. He is holy.*

Adapted from Psalms 96 and 99.

Leader Let us perfect holiness out of reverence for God.

Group *We have been set apart to be God's holy people.*

Meditation and listening to God

Thought for meditation:

I will find my highest personal holiness when I lose myself in a desire to extol the worth, reputation, honour and splendour of God the Father, God the Son and God the Holy Spirit.

from *Let the Light Shine* by Derek Osborne.

To close:

Leader You shall be holy unto me because I the Lord am holy.

Prayer and praise

Worship songs

All to Jesus I surrender
J. W. Van De Venter

All to Jesus I surrender,
all to him I freely give;
I will ever love and trust him,
in his presence daily live.

I surrender all, I surrender all,
all to thee, my blessed Saviour
I surrender all.

All to Jesus I surrender,
humbly at his feet I bow;
worldly pleasures all forsaken,
take me, Jesus, take me now.

All to Jesus I surrender,
make me, Saviour, wholly thine;
let me feel the Holy Spirit,
truly know that thou art mine.

All to Jesus I surrender,
Lord, I give myself to thee;
fill me with thy love and power,
let thy blessing fall on me.

Continued over

All to Jesus I surrender,
now to feel the sacred flame;
O, the joy of full salvation!
Glory, glory to his name.

© HarperCollins Religious/CopyCare

Purify my heart
Brian Doerksen

Purify my heart,
let me be as gold and precious silver.
Purify my heart,
let me be as gold, pure gold.

Refiner's fire,
my heart's desire
is to be holy,
set apart for you, Lord.
I choose to be holy,
set apart for you, my Master,
ready to do your will.

Purify my heart,
cleanse me from within and make me holy.
Purify my heart,
cleanse me from my sin, deep within.

© 1990 Mercy/Vineyard Publishing/CopyCare

Prayer

Members of the group read the following verses in turn to express their worship of a holy God. The group respond with the phrase given after each reading. Spontaneous prayers may continue after the readings.

Leader The Lord is my strength and my song;
he has become my salvation.
He is my God and I will praise him,
my father's God and I will exalt him.
Who among the gods is like you, O Lord?
Who is like you – majestic in holiness, awesome in glory, working wonders?
The Lord will reign for ever and ever.

Exodus 15:2, 11, 18

Group *Amen. You are holy, Lord.*

Leader Ascribe to the Lord, O mighty ones,
ascribe to the Lord glory and strength.
Ascribe to the Lord the glory due to his name.
Worship the Lord in the splendour of his holiness.

Psalm 29:1, 2

Group *Amen. You are holy, Lord.*

Leader Be exalted, O God, above the heavens; let your glory be over all the earth.
For great is your love, reaching to the heavens;
your faithfulness reaches to the skies.
I cry out to God, most high,
to God who fulfils his purpose for me.

Psalm 57:11, 10, 2

Group *Amen. You are holy, Lord.*

Leader Shout with joy to God, all the earth!
Sing to the glory of his name!
Offer Him glory and praise!
Say to God, 'How awesome are your deeds!'
Come and see what God has done,
how awesome his works on our behalf!

Psalm 66:1-3, 5

Group *Amen. You are holy, Lord.*

Leader O Lord my God, you are very great;
you are clothed with splendour and majesty.
May the glory of the Lord endure forever;
may the Lord rejoice in his works.
May my meditation be pleasing to him,
as I rejoice in the Lord.

Psalm 104:1, 31, 34

Group *Amen. You are holy, Lord.*

Leader Give thanks to the Lord, call on his name;
make known among the nations what he has done.
Glory in his holy name,
let the hearts of those who seek the Lord rejoice.
Look to the Lord and his strength;
seek his face always.

Psalm 105:1, 3, 4

Group *Amen. You are holy, Lord.*

Leader Not unto us, O Lord, not unto us,
but to your name be the glory,
because of your love and faithfulness.

The highest heavens belong to the Lord,
but the earth, he has given to mankind.

Psalm 115:1, 16

Group *Amen. You are holy, Lord.*

Leader Great is the Lord and most worthy of praise;
his greatness no one can fathom.
His kingdom is an everlasting kingdom
and his dominion endures through all generations.
The Lord is faithful to all his promises
and loving towards all He has made.
My mouth will speak in praise of the Lord.
Let every creature praise his holy name
for ever and ever.

Psalm 145:3, 13, 21

Group *Amen. You are holy, Lord.*

Leader Lord, I have heard of your glory.
I stand in awe of your deeds, O Lord.
Renew them in our day,
in our own time make them known;
in wrath, remember mercy.

Habakkuk 3:2

Group *Amen. You are holy, Lord.*

Leader Holy, holy, holy is the Lord God Almighty,
who was, and is, and is to come.
You are worthy, our Lord and God,
to receive glory and honour and power,
for you created all things
and by your will they were created and have their being.

Revelation 4:8b, 11

Group *Amen. You are holy, Lord.*

Leader To him who sits on the throne and to the Lamb
be praise and honour and glory and power,
for ever and ever.

Revelation 5:13b

Group *Amen. You are holy, Lord.*

Further activity

Holiness: Three Key Words

Acceptance: being sure of adoptive status.   (GOD)

Obligation: taking responsibilities seriously.   (JESUS)

Enablement: to do and to be.   (HOLY SPIRIT)

Closing words

Holiness comes from being secure as a child of God,

living like Christ in grace and truth,

proving God's truth by having faith in the Holy Spirit

and giving God the glory. Amen.

Only by grace

Words and Music: Gerrit Gustafson

© Copyright 1990 Integrity's Hosanna! Music. Administered by Kingsway's
Thankyou Music, P.O. Box 75, Eastbourne, East Sussex, BN23 6NW, UK. (For the UK only.) Used by permission.

All to Jesus I surrender
I surrender all

Words: J.W. Van De Venter
Music: W. S. Weedon

Words © Copyright HarperCollins Religious. Administered by CopyCare,
P.O. Box 77, Hailsham, East Sussex, BN27 3EF, UK. (music@copycare.com) Used by permission.

2. All to Jesus I surrender,
   humbly at his feet I bow;
   worldly pleasures all forsaken,
   take me, Jesus, take me now.

3. All to Jesus I surrender,
   make me, Saviour, wholly thine;
   let me feel the Holy Spirit,
   truly know that thou art mine.

4. All to Jesus I surrender,
   Lord, I give myself to thee;
   fill me with thy love and power,
   let thy blessing fall on me.

5. All to Jesus I surrender,
   now to feel the sacred flame;
   O, the joy of full salvation!
   Glory, glory to his name!

Purify my heart
Refiner's fire

Words and Music: Brian Doerksen

© Copyright 1990 Mercy/Vineyard Publishing/Music Services. Administered by CopyCare,
P.O. Box 77, Hailsham, East Sussex, BN27, 3EF, UK. (music@copycare.com) Used by permission.

2. Purify my heart,
   cleanse me from within and make me holy.
   Purify my heart,
   cleanse me from my sin, deep within.

SESSION 4

Notes for Leader

Session 4: Family Worship

THEME: CHILDREN OF OUR HEAVENLY FATHER

Introduction to theme

This may seem a difficult theme in which to involve adults, as they may assume that the songs, prayers and activities are only directed at the children. Yet Jesus himself suggested that we have to understand how to worship as a child, in a simple way, in order to find the Kingdom of God.

Not everyone in the group will enjoy modelling with playdough or drawing pictures, but they may not mind talking about childhood memories!

Keep it simple, involve children in the meeting and encourage the adults to learn from them. Get some families involved in preparation beforehand, for example, with the prayers.

Resources required

You will need enough copies of the session for your group.

Worship songs

These will be found on Album 1, tracks 13-16.

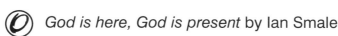 *God is here, God is present* by Ian Smale

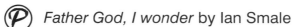 *Father God, I wonder* by Ian Smale

I'm your child by Richard Hubbard

 Meditation track – *Enchantment*

A lump of playdough or plasticine for each person for the activity

 For alternative activities (see page 95), you will need:

- Pictures of children from magazines/catalogues

- Large sheet of newsprint or wallpaper (plain newsprint paper can usually be obtained in large end-rolls from newspaper printers free of charge)

- Glue sticks

- Photographs of people in the group, taken when they were children

- A long piece of paper for the clues to the verse (see page 98).

Preparation

 Meditation and listening to God

Thought for meditation:

Leader The disciples came to Jesus and asked, 'Who is the greatest in the Kingdom of Heaven?' He called a little child and had him stand among them. And he said, 'I tell you the truth, unless you change and become like little children, you will never enter the Kingdom of Heaven. . .   And whoever welcomes a little child like this, in my name, welcomes me.'

Matthew 18:1-5

Jesus said, 'Let the little children come to me and do not hinder them, for the Kingdom of God belongs to such as these. I tell you the truth, anyone who will not receive the Kingdom of God like a little child will never enter it.' And he took the children in his arms, put his hands on them and blessed them.

Mark 10:13-16

I was once a child
but now I am grown,
I need to be shown.

I was once happy
just to trust;
now proof is a must!

I used to believe
what I could not see;
how could that be?

I used to follow
wherever you'd go;
now I need to know.

Pat Turner

Suggested time 2 minutes.

Before moving on, allow time for the group to share any thoughts arising from the time of meditation.

 Prayer and praise

The prayer by Jo Pimlott could be followed by an opportunity for the children to pray, thanking God, or praying for specific needs of the group. Families could come prepared with prayers written by their children.

You could teach the children a simple format for prayer (it also works for adults!) using the picture of 'praying hands' on page 97. Start with both hands in front of you, clenched in fists. As the children repeat each line of the rhyme, they open up their fingers into 'praying hands'.

Thumbs up to worship Father and Son.

This finger's sorry for bad things I've done.

This finger thanks God for all I see,

and this finger says, 'Bless you and me.'

The little ones make two hands that pray:

'God, I want to serve and love you today.'

Devised by Margaret Inkpen

Between the two worship songs, suggest a group member reads the poem by Jane Amey.

 Further activity

Use some of the following questions to develop discussion.

- What did Jesus mean by 'becoming as a child', or to 'humble oneself like a child'?
- What does it mean to be a child when one has grown up?
- What is the difference between being 'childlike' and 'childish'?
- How can we receive the Kingdom like a little child?
- What are the qualities of little children that Jesus liked, which may be lost in an adult?
- How can God use children to serve him?

Look at some of the children in the Bible. God was at work in their lives. Get the children involved by finding out what they know about these young people. Write the names below on cards and hold them up for everyone to see.

ISAAC

- Who were his father and mother?
- What did God ask Abraham to do with his son, Isaac?

God said that through Abraham's son all the nations would be blessed.

JACOB AND ESAU

- What was special about these two brothers?

The Lord answered Isaac's prayer. His wife Rebekah couldn't have children, but when Isaac prayed, the Lord gave her twins. They were God's answer to prayer.

JOSEPH

- What did Joseph's father give him because he was the favourite son?
- What did Joseph do that made his brothers hate him?

God had a plan for Joseph and because he could interpret dreams, he became an important person in Egypt and saved his family from starvation.

SAMUEL

Another baby who was an answer to prayer.

- Where did Samuel grow up, because of his mother's promise?
- What was the name of the priest who brought Samuel up in the temple?
- What happened to Samuel one night?

God didn't think Samuel too young to take a message for him. Samuel grew up to be a prophet and knew God's voice, but he started when he was very young.

DAVID

- Where was David when Samuel went to find him?
- What musical instrument did David play?
- What else did David do?

God knew David's heart and chose him to be a king when he was still young and only a shepherd boy. God knows our potential.

NAAMAN'S SLAVE GIRL

- What did she do for Naaman?

She is not given a name in the Bible, but she cared very much for her master, and she believed in God for healing. A little slave girl had great faith and could teach a bunch of soldiers about God.

BOY WITH LOAVES AND FISHES

- How many people did Jesus feed with the loaves and fishes?

This little boy didn't have very much, but maybe he just wanted to share his food with Jesus. He probably never imagined it would be used for a miracle. If we give what we have to Jesus, who knows what he will use it for!

JAIRUS' DAUGHTER

- What happened to her?

I wonder what she felt when she woke up? We know she was hungry because Jesus told her family to give her some food. Her dad loved her so much that he pushed his way through a big crowd to reach Jesus. He believed Jesus could heal her. Children are very special to Jesus.

Creative activity

Give each person in the group a lump of playdough or plasticine. The group is divided into pairs. Children can be part of family groups or work together. Each person is asked to make a model of their partner, thinking of how God created everybody with unique differences. Some people may prefer to draw a picture of their partner, or just talk to each other, finding out special aspects of their character or childhood.

To close, suggest that each person pray for the partner they have modelled or drawn, thanking God for the qualities and gifts they have been given.

 Alternative suggestions for creative activities:

Photographs of childhood

With prior planning, members of the group bring photos of themselves as children. In small groups they then share their experiences and memories.

- Did they go to church or Sunday school?
- What do they remember learning about God, Jesus or the Bible?
- Do they remember being afraid?
- Who did they trust or admire?

Children's mural

Using cut-out pictures of babies and children, build up a mural on a large sheet of paper, wallpaper or even a large cardboard box. (This can stand on its own without needing to be fixed to a wall!) With glue sticks, children can stick pictures to the box or paper and also attach their written prayers.

Solving the verse

Using a long piece of paper or wallpaper, draw the picture clues for the verse to be solved (Psalm 8:2). Using a thick black felt pen, fill in the words, as the young people work out each clue. Two people will be needed to hold either end of the paper.

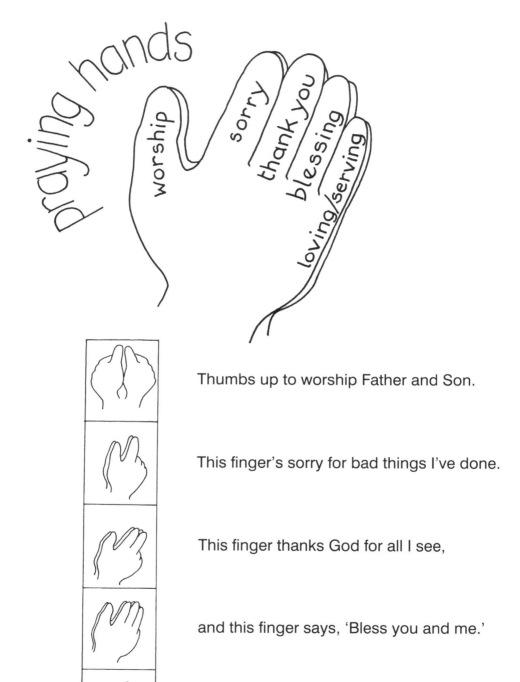

praying hands

worship · sorry · thank you · blessing · loving/serving

Thumbs up to worship Father and Son.

This finger's sorry for bad things I've done.

This finger thanks God for all I see,

and this finger says, 'Bless you and me.'

The little ones make two hands that pray:
'God, I want to serve and love you today.'

Solve the verse

Psalm 8:2

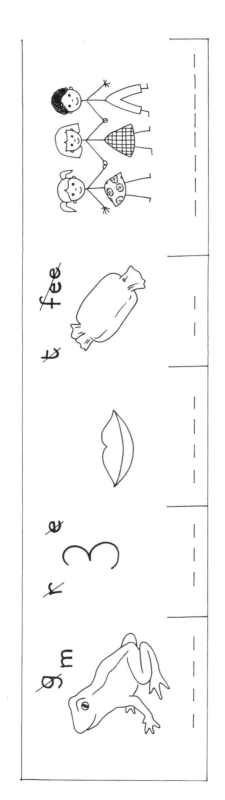

Worship Session 4

THEME: CHILDREN OF OUR HEAVENLY FATHER

Opening words

Leader How great is the love the Father has lavished on us, that we should be called children of God! And that is what we are!

1 John 3:1a

Group *Thank you, Lord, that we are all your children.*

Worship song

God is here, God is present
Ian Smale

God is here, God is present,
God is moving by his Spirit.
Can you hear what he is saying,
are you willing to respond?
God is here, God is present,
God is moving by his Spirit.
Lord, I open up my life to you,
please do just what you will.

Lord, I won't stop loving you,
You mean more to me than anyone else.
Lord, I won't stop loving you,
you mean more to me than anyone else.

© 1987 Kingsway's Thankyou Music

Reading from the Psalms

Leader O Lord, you have searched me and you know me.
You know when I sit and when I rise;
you perceive my thoughts from afar.

Group member You discern my going out and my lying down;
you are familiar with all my ways.
Before a word is on my tongue,
you know it completely, O Lord.

Group *O Lord, you have searched me and you know me.*

Leader You hem me in, behind and before;
you have laid Your hand upon me.
Such knowledge is too wonderful for me,
too lofty for me to attain.

Group member Where can I go from your Spirit?
Where can I flee from your presence?
If I go up to the heavens, you are there;
if I make my bed in the depths, you are there.
If I rise on the wings of the dawn,
if I settle on the far side of the sea,
even there your hand will guide me,
your right hand will hold me fast.

Group *O Lord, you have searched me and you know me.*

Leader If I say, 'Surely the darkness will hide me
and the light become night around me',
even the darkness will not be dark to you;
the night will shine like the day,
for darkness is as light to you.

Group *O Lord, you have searched me and you know me.*

Group member You created my inmost being;
you knit me together in my mother's womb.
I praise you because I am fearfully and wonderfully
made.
Your works are wonderful, I know that full well.

Group *O Lord, you have searched me and you know me.*
All the days ordained for me were written in your book
before one of them came to be.
How precious to me are your thoughts, O God!

Psalm 139:1–17

Leader How great is the love the Father has lavished on us,
that we should be called children of God!
And that is what we are.

Group *Thank you, Lord, that we are all your children.*

Meditation and listening to God

Thought for meditation:

Leader The disciples came to Jesus and asked, 'Who is the greatest in the Kingdom of Heaven?' He called a little child and had him stand among them. And he said, 'I tell you the truth, unless you change and become like little children, you will never enter the Kingdom of Heaven. . . And whoever welcomes a little child like this, in my name, welcomes me.'

Matthew 18:1-5

Jesus said, 'Let the little children come to me and do not hinder them, for the Kingdom of God belongs to such as these. I tell you the truth, anyone who will not receive the Kingdom of God like a little child will never enter it.' And he took the children in his arms, put his hands on them and blessed them.

Mark 10:13-16

I was once a child
but now I am grown,
I need to be shown.

I was once happy
just to trust;
now proof is a must!

I used to believe
what I could not see;
how could that be?

I used to follow
wherever you'd go;
now I need to know.

Pat Turner

To close

Leader Anyone who will not receive the Kingdom of God like a child will never enter it.

Prayer and praise

Leader and group read this prayer together:

Father God,

give us joy to laugh as children laugh.

Give us eyes to see as children see.

Give us hope to dream as children dream.

Give us boldness to ask as children ask.

Give us curiosity to seek as children seek.

Give us humility to learn as children learn.

Give us faith to trust as children trust.

Give us grace not to be childish – but childlike,

for your glory.

Amen.

Jo Pimlott

Worship songs

Father God, I wonder
Ian Smale

Father God, I wonder
how I managed to exist
without the knowledge of your parenthood
and your loving care.
But now I am your child,
I am adopted in your family
and I can never be alone
'cause, Father God, you're there beside me.

I will sing your praises,
I will sing your praises,
I will sing your praises
for ever more.
I will sing your praises,
I will sing your praises,
I will sing your praises
for ever more.

© 1984 Kingsway's Thankyou Music

Poem: *His Child*, by Jane Amey

Created in his image,
tenderly adored,
forgiven of my sinful past
and lovingly restored.

Intimately known to him,
secure in his embrace,
the Father's child reflecting
the glory of his face.

Walking in his footsteps,
obedience is my aim –
to make the Father smile with joy
and hear him call my name.

Never will he leave me –
his love is guaranteed.
When Jesus bled for all of us
his children Father freed.

I'm your child
Richard Hubbard

I'm your child and you are my God.

I thank You, Father, for your loving care.

I'm your child and you are my God.

You've made me special and you're always there.

I'm your child and you are my God.

I love you, Jesus; you're close to me.

I'm your child and you are my God.

I give you worship, I bow the knee.

I'm your child and you are my God.

Holy Spirit, flow through me.

I'm your child and you are my God.

You give me power and authority.

© 1991 Kingsway's Thankyou Music

Leader You are the children of the Lord your God. The Lord has chosen you to be his treasured possession.

Deuteronomy 14:1a, 2b

Further activity

Look at some of the children in the Bible and see how God was at work in their lives.

ISAAC

- Who were his father and mother?
- What did God ask Abraham to do with his son?

JACOB AND ESAU

- What was special about these two brothers?

JOSEPH

- What did Joseph's father give him because he was the favourite son?
- What did Joseph do to make his brothers hate him?

SAMUEL
– another baby who was an answer to prayer

- Where did Samuel grow up, because of his mother's promise?
- What was the name of the priest who brought Samuel up?
- What happened to Samuel one night?

DAVID

- Where was David when Samuel went to find him?
- What musical instrument did David play?
- What else did David do?

NAAMAN'S SLAVE GIRL

- What did she do for Naaman?

BOY WITH LOAVES AND FISHES

- How many people did Jesus feed with the loaves and fishes?

JAIRUS' DAUGHTER

- What happened to her?

Children are very special to Jesus.

Closing words

Father God,

help us to see other people as you see them,

recognising that they are created by you

for a special purpose and that you love them.

We are all your children

and we want to come to you as children,

in childlike simplicity, with childlike faith.

We offer our worship to you

and say that we love you

as children coming to a wonderful Father.

Accept us just as we are, Lord God.

Amen.

God is here, God is present

Words and Music: Ian Smale

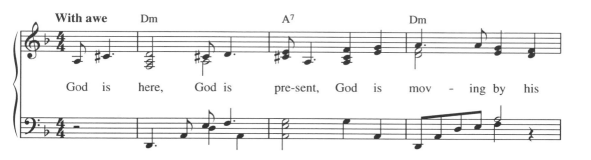

God is here, God is pre-sent, God is mov - ing by his

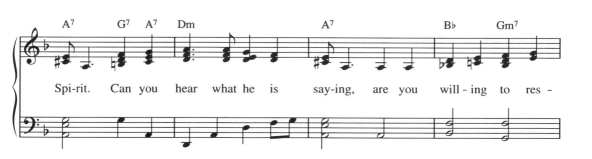

Spi-rit. Can you hear what he is say-ing, are you will - ing to res -

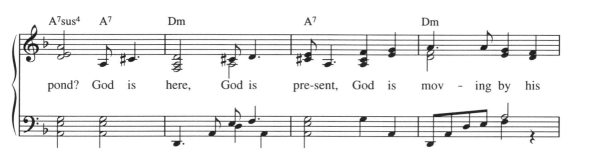

pond? God is here, God is pre-sent, God is mov - ing by his

Spi - rit. Lord, I o – pen up my life to you, please

© Copyright 1987 Kingsway's Thankyou Music, P.O. Box 75, Eastbourne,
East Sussex, BN23 6NW, UK. Used by permission.

Father God, I wonder
I will sing your praises

Words and Music: Ian Smale

© Copyright 1984 Kingsway's Thankyou Music, P.O. Box 75, Eastbourne,
East Sussex, BN23 6NW, UK. Used by permission.

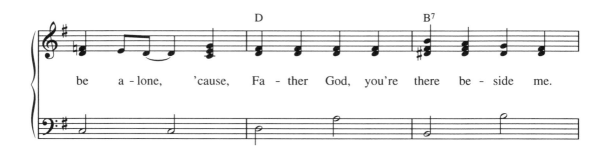

be a - lone, 'cause, Fa - ther God, you're there be - side me.

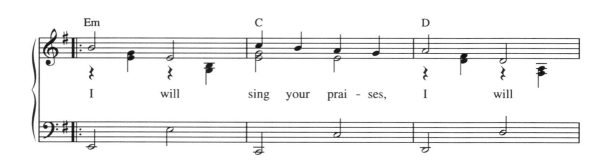

I will sing your prai - ses, I will

sing your prai - ses, I will sing your prai - ses,

for e - ver - more. for e - ver - more.

I'm your child

Words and Music: Richard Hubbard

2. I'm your child and you are my God.
   I love you Jesus, you're close to me.
   I'm your child and you are my God.
   I give you worship, I bow the knee.

3. I'm your child and you are my God.
   Holy Spirit, flow out to me.
   I'm your child and you are my God.
   You give me power and authority.

© Copyright 1991 Kingsway's Thankyou Music, P.O. Box 75, Eastbourne,
East Sussex, BN23 6NW, UK. Used by permission.

SESSION 5

Notes for Leader

Session 5: Social Awareness and Specific Issues

THEME: ACCEPTANCE

Introduction to theme

Acceptance starts with oneself. It is easy to acknowledge in prayers and readings that we are loved by God and accepted 'for who we are'; difficult, maybe, to believe it.

Before we embark on evangelistic strategies and acts of goodness, assuring people that they are worth Jesus' death, that God loves the sinner, the outcast, the millionaire, we need to be certain of that ourselves. The stones/pebbles (see Meditation section) serve as physical examples.

This may be a difficult subject, but it gives plenty of food for thought. The sketch provides an informal basis for discussion, and the cuttings of recent or local news can give direction to prayers and worship.

Resources required

You will need enough copies of the session for your group.

Worship songs

These will be found on Album 1, tracks 17-20.

 Jesus, take me as I am by Dave Bryant

 There is none like you by Lenny LeBlanc

 Your mercy flows by Wes Sutton

 Meditation track – *My friend*

A selection of stones and pebbles, one of which should be a cut gemstone such as an amethyst (available from a rock shop) or a small piece of jewellery with a gemstone in it.

 Cuttings from newspapers concerning issues of social injustice, suffering, discrimination, social problems and suchlike.

 5 copies of the script for the sketch *Ticket to Heaven*.

 A large sheet of paper headed 'Equal Opportunities' and a felt pen.

Preparation

 Meditation and listening to God

As you share the introductory words of the meditation with the group, pick up one of the stones or pebbles for each of the characters mentioned. The last one should be the gemstone – precious, which is how God sees us.

Ask a member of the group to read Pat Turner's poem, *If only you knew*.

Tell each group member to choose a stone or pebble to hold as they meditate.

Suggested time for meditation: 3-5 minutes.

Before moving on, allow time for the group to share any thoughts arising from the time of meditation.

Further activity

The sketch *Ticket to Heaven*, can be used as a basis for discussion. You could perform it if you have a few people who enjoy drama and can give time for 2-3 rehearsals; otherwise the parts can be read by people in the group, possibly going through it twice to understand the thought behind it.

For the discussion

Address issues of acceptance:

• What does Jesus see in people?

• What are the general public's ideas of a Christian?

• Who gets to heaven?

The characters can be discussed:

• Who did you like?

• Who did you have problems relating to?

• What would you have said in a similar situation?

When you have finished judging others, look at people you know and discuss openly what you feel about being accepted, who is more important, more gifted, etc.

• Would we feel able to accept 'the ticket'?

Discuss the questions on acceptance with the group, using a large sheet of paper to make a list from examples given by the group, under heading 'Equal Opportunities'.

TICKET TO HEAVEN
Pat Turner

The cast

Goody	a genuinely good person
Hero	boastful, large muscles
Just me	low self-esteem
Brains	clever and knows it!
Jesus	

Props

Four tickets saying HEAVEN and a table

A sign 'SPECIAL PERSONS' CONFERENCE'

A badge with 'Mummy's Little Helper' on it

(Just me seems to be out of the action, at the back. Goody is seated separately. Hero is in the middle of boasting)

Hero The heat was intense (wipes away the sweat) . . . but there was no time to lose. It was time for – a HERO *(He poses heroically)* – so I ran into the house and pulled the child out of the raging inferno.

(He walks away, proud and expecting adoration. Instead, Brains merely thinks aloud)

Brains Mmm. A blaze like that must have needed fifty cubic metres of water . . . and using Pythagoras for the length of the ladder . . .

(Hero is dumbfounded)

Brains . . . coupled with 'speed equals distance over time', I calculate you had ten seconds to escape from the top window, leaving only one second before the roof collapsed.

*(**Hero** is staring at him; mouth wide open)*

Hero Exactly.

Brains *(Congratulates himself)* I always was good at Maths . . .

Just me *(Tries to be friendly)* I wish I was like you. Maths is a complete mystery to me . . . so is German, and History, and . . .

(They slowly turn to look at him. He dries up and retreats. They carry on)

Hero What can I say? It takes someone special to do a rescue like that. I have the strength, I have the guts – oh, and naturally, I also have the girls.

*(He poses, flexing his muscles. **Just me** tries to copy him, looking for muscles, but he can't find any!)*

Just me *(Sighs)* I wish I was like you.

Hero *(Irritated)* Excuse me, I don't seem to know your name.

Just me Oh, Just . . .

Brains Justin

Just me No, Just . . .

Brains Don't tell me. I'll get it.
(Racks his brain) Just . . . Just . . .

Just me Just me!

Brains *(Shakes head)* Doesn't ring a bell. What have you done?

Just me Nothing.

Goody You must have done something! This is the 'Someone Special' conference.

Just me I'm not special! I'm . . . well . . . ordinary, really.

Hero Not special? Why are you here then?

*(**Hero** and **Brains** take a menacing step closer)*

Just me *(Embarrassed)* Well, I . . . I . . . I was given an invitation.

*(Awkward pause. He looks at **Hero** and **Brains**)*

Just me Probably a mistake. *(He backs away from them)* I'll just sit at the back. You won't know I'm here, honest.

(They have already forgotten about him and are in a private discussion. Eventually freeze)

Just me I'll just . . . blend into the background.

*(**Goody** sidles over to join **Just me**)*

Goody To tell you the truth, I don't feel special either. I'm just good, really. 'Goody-goody' *(He laughs, embarrassed)* Do as you are told; be kind to everyone . . . It's hard work being good all the time. Take football yesterday . . . This kid came straight at me with the ball and my team shouted, 'TACKLE HIM!' . . . but I had to let him go past!

Just me Why?

Goody He said, 'Excuse me, please!' . . . so I stood aside and let him through. He scored a goal.

Just me Never mind. Being good must be very rewarding.

Goody That's the trouble! I washed the pots last night and got a reward.

Just me What was it?

*(**Goody** looks around before producing large badge - 'Mummy's little helper'. Deep embarrassment)*

Just me I wish I was like you. I've never had a reward! I'm not clever, I'm not brave, I'm not even good! I'm so ordinary! I'm fed up of being Just me.

*(**Jesus** enters with the tickets to Heaven!)*

Jesus Friends! Glad you could come. Here they are . . . *(waves the tickets)* tickets for all the special people.

*(**Hero** and **Brains** are expecting attention. **Jesus** hands a ticket to **Just me**)*

Jesus This one's for you.

*(**Just me** looks at it . . . a ticket to Heaven!)*

Just me *(Jumps up)* A ticket to Heaven! *(Shows the audience)* IT'S A TICKET TO HEAVEN!

*(He looks at **Hero** and **Brains**, who are glaring at him)*

Just me There must be some mistake!

Jesus *(Hand on his shoulder)* You're special to me.

*(Just me holds the ticket tightly. **Jesus** puts the other tickets on a table and moves to go)*

Brains *(Complains)* Hey! What has he done to deserve that?

Jesus Nothing.

Brains It's blatant favouritism. What about us?

Jesus Oh yes. *(He indicates to the table)* There's yours.

*(**Jesus** and **Just me** leave)*

Hero Wait! You haven't told us what to do!
(They have gone. He asks the others)
What do we have to do?

Goody *(Has been observing)* Pick it up.

Brains   Pick it up? Just PICK IT UP?

I've never been so insulted. I've spent years . . . years! Studying, sweating, revising, all for bits of paper. *(Substitute your own brand of qualifications)* Ten GCSEs, six 'A' levels, a degree . . . My swimming certificate! I've worked long and hard for these . . . and he thinks I'm just going to 'pick it up'? No thank you!

(He storms off)

Goody   *(Picks one up. Notices the name on it)* Oh, sorry. This one's yours.

*(**Hero** jabs him playfully, dancing with fancy footwork, ready for boxing)*

Hero   Put 'em up. Put 'em up.

Goody   What?

*(**Hero** jabs him again)*

Hero   I'll fight you for it.

Goody   I don't want to fight. *(Holds it out)* Look, it's yours. It's got your name on it.

Hero   Come on! . . . An arm-wrestle then. I bet I win in three seconds.

Goody   I bet I get a broken wrist! No thank you!

Hero   Spoilsport. All right then. What do you want me to do? Climb a mountain? Swim a river? Fight a lion with my bare hands?

Goody Take the ticket! *(Holds it out)*

*(**Hero** is exasperated. Hands go to his head, then fall to the sides)*

Hero What's brave about that?

*(Frustrated. Shakes head and leaves. **Goody** puts **Hero's** ticket down and picks up his own. Talks to himself)*

Goody Take the ticket. *(Looks at it. Puts it in his pocket. Makes to go. Stops. Takes the ticket out. Stares at it and shakes head)* Heaven! Wow! That's quite a reward. I mean . . . Paradise! . . . Eternal Life and all that. Whew! *(Thinks)* If I could get to Heaven . . . *(Realises)* Well, I can! . . . I mean, I've got the ticket, haven't I? *(Puts it in his pocket and makes to go again. Stops)* No, it's no good. I can't. *(Takes ticket out of pocket and looks at it)* I mean, how good do you have to be, to get to Heaven? *(Shakes his head sadly and puts the ticket down)* Better than me . . . *(He walks off)*

Worship Session 5

THEME: ACCEPTANCE

Opening words

Leader Jesus told this parable: 'Two men went up to the temple to pray, one a Pharisee and the other a tax collector. The Pharisee stood up and prayed about himself: "God, I thank you that I am not like other men – robbers, evildoers, adulterers – or even like this tax collector. I fast twice a week and give a tenth of all I get."

But the tax collector stood at a distance. He would not even look up to heaven, but beat his breast and said, "God, have mercy on me, a sinner".

I tell you that this man (the tax collector) went home justified before God. For everyone who exalts himself will be humbled, and he who humbles himself will be exalted.'

Luke 18:10-14

Group *Show me your ways, O Lord,*
guide me in Your truth and teach me.
According to your love, remember me.

From Psalm 25

Leader This is what the Almighty says: 'Administer true justice; show mercy and compassion to one another.
In your hearts do not think evil of each other.'

Zechariah 7:9, 10b

Group *Show me your ways, O Lord,*
guide me in Your truth and teach me.
According to your love, remember me.

From Psalm 25

Worship song

Jesus, take me as I am
Dave Bryant

Jesus, take me as I am,

I can come no other way.

Take me deeper into you,

make my flesh life die away.

Make me like a precious stone,

crystal clear and finely honed.

Life of Jesus shining through,

giving glory back to you.

© 1978 Kingsway's Thankyou Music

(During the singing, the leader places the stones and pebbles on a central table, at least one for each member of the group.)

Reading from the Psalms

Leader I will exalt you, my God the King;
I will praise your name for ever and ever.

Group *Everyday I will praise you*
and extol your name for ever and ever.

(A member of the group reads a newspaper cutting about a situation in which there is suffering, discrimination, injustice or social problems.)

Leader Great is the Lord and most worthy of praise;
His greatness no one can fathom.

Group *I will meditate on your wonderful works;*
I will proclaim your great deeds.

(Another member of the group reads a newspaper article.)

Leader The Lord is gracious and compassionate,
slow to anger and rich in love.

Group *The Lord is good to all;*
he has compassion on all he has made.
All you have made will praise you, O Lord.

(Another member of the group reads a newspaper article.)

Leader The Lord is faithful to all his promises,
and loving towards all he has made.

Group *The Lord upholds all those who fall,*
and lifts up all who are bowed down.

(Another member of the group reads a newspaper article.)

Leader You open your hand
and satisfy the desires of every living thing.

Group *The Lord is righteous in all his ways,*
and loving towards all he has made.

(Another member of the group reads a newspaper article.)

Leader The Lord is near to all who call on Him,
to all who call on him in truth.

Group *He fulfils the desires of those who fear him;*
He hears their cry and saves them.

(Another member of the group reads a newspaper article.)

Leader The Lord watches over all who love him,
but all the wicked he will destroy.

Group *My mouth will speak in praise of the Lord.*
Let every creature praise his holy name for ever and
ever.

From Psalm 145

Note If there are more newspaper articles to be read out than verses above, insert more than one at each point in the Psalm.

Meditation and listening to God

Thought for meditation:

Leader God's ways are not our ways, his thoughts are not our thoughts. God looks on the inside; we only see the outside.

Joseph's brothers thought he would be the last man to be God's choice: precocious, proud, and irritating.

Look at Moses – yes! He had power and prestige to add to the Hebrew cause – but he had to spend forty years in the wilderness before he could be useful to God.

David – just a boy out with the sheep

Esther – an orphaned exile

Gideon – a nobody

Fishermen, tax collectors, rich rulers, lepers – no, definitely not our choice for positions of importance.

But God looks from a different perspective; he sees each one of us – chosen, special, worth the price.

Do you believe it?

Poem: *If only you knew* by Pat Turner

If only you knew what was offered today;
if only you knew the life-giving water,
the cleansing, refreshing, peaceful water.
If only you knew who was talking to you;
if only you knew.

If only you knew.

If only you knew what he gave for your life;
if only you knew why he came.
If only you knew how he longs in his heart,
how he aches, as he reaches to you;
if only you knew.

If only you knew.

If only you knew the joy of his love,
his security, friendship and peace,
his beauty, his holiness shines like the sun,
he radiates life and release.

You can be who you are,
not be . . . what you do,
if only you knew.

(Each member of the group chooses a stone or pebble from the collection to hold as they meditate.)

To close

Leader Do not judge, and you will not be judged.
Do not condemn and you will not be condemned.
Forgive and you will be forgiven.
Give, and it shall be given to you. A good measure,
pressed down, shaken together and running over.
With the measure you use, it will be measured to you.

Luke 6:37, 38

Prayer and praise

Worship songs

Your mercy flows
Wes Sutton

Your mercy flows upon us like a river.
Your mercy stands unshakeable and true.
Most Holy God, of all good things the giver,
we turn and lift our fervent prayer to you.

Hear our cry (hear our cry),
Lord (O Lord),
be merciful (be merciful)
once more (once more).
Let your love (let your love)
your anger stem (your anger stem),
remember mercy, O Lord, again.

© 1987 Sovereign Lifestyle Music Ltd

There is none like you
Lenny LeBlanc

There is none like you,

no one else can touch my heart like you do.

I could search for all eternity long

and find there is none like you.

Your mercy flows like a river wide,

and healing comes from your hands.

Suffering children are safe in your arms;

there is none like you.

© *1991 Integrity's Hosanna! Music/Kingsway's Thankyou Music*

Prayer

Group *(Reading together)*

Lord;
hold us back when we want to judge.

We want to change people from the outside
but you change people from the inside.

You know them completely
and love them completely.
They can come to you
at any time,
just as they are
and find acceptance in you.

And you accept me too.

Pat Turner

Continue in prayer for specific situations and people,
for members of the group, for yourselves. Thank God
for his love and acceptance of you, with all your weaknesses and faults; thank him for opportunities to care
for people around you and pray for opportunities to
share his love.

Further activity

Discussion based on the sketch *Ticket to Heaven* by Pat Turner.

Leader (after discussion)

While we were still sinners,
Christ died for us.

Romans 5:8

Whoever is thirsty, let him come;
and whoever wishes, let him take
the free gift of the water of life.

Revelation 22:17

How can we share this 'acceptance by Jesus' with those who feel rejected by society?

Can you think of situations in the Bible where Jesus accepted 'outcasts', or showed friendship to people who you find surprising? (Rich, poor, leper, thief, 'sinner', etc.)

Closing words

Do not judge or you too will be judged. For in the same way as you judge others, you will be judged, and with the measure you use, it will be measured to you. Why do you look at the speck of sawdust in your brother's eye and pay no attention to the plank in your own eye? . . . First take the plank out of your own eye, and then you will see clearly to remove the speck from your brother's eye.

Matthew 7:1–5

If anyone is without sin, let him be the first to throw a stone?

John 8:7

Group *(spoken)* *Make me a precious stone*
crystal clear and finely honed.
Life of Jesus shining through,
giving glory back to you.

Amen.

N.B. Take your stone or pebble home with you!

Jesus, take me as I am

Words and Music: Dave Bryant

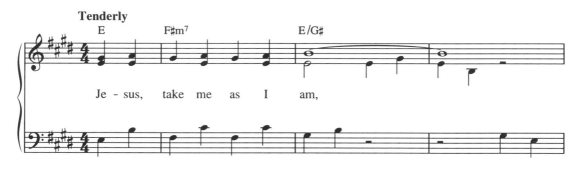

Je-sus, take me as I am,

I can come no o-ther way.

Take me deep-er in-to you,

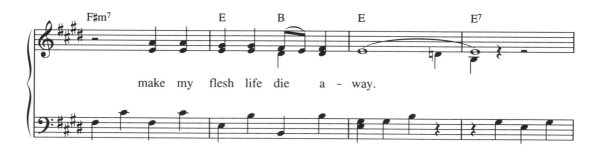

make my flesh life die a - way.

© Copyright 1978 Kingsway's Thankyou Music, P.O. Box 75, Eastbourne, East Sussex, BN23 6NW, UK. Used by permission.

Make me like a pre-cious stone,

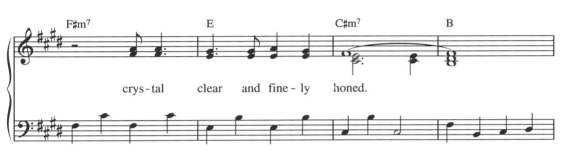

crys-tal clear and fine-ly honed.

Life of Je - sus shin-ing through,

giv-ing glo - ry back to you.

Your mercy flows

Words and Music: Wes Sutton

© Copyright 1987 Sovereign Lifestyle Music Ltd, P.O. Box 356,
Leighton Buzzard, Bedfordshire, LU7 8WP, UK. Used by permission.

2. Your church once great, though standing clothed in sorrow,
   is even still the bride that you adore;
   revive your church, that we again may honour
   our God and King, our Master and our Lord.

3. As we have slept, this nation has been taken
   by ev'ry sin we have ever known,
   so at its gates, though burnt by fire and broken,
   in Jesus' name we come to take our stand.

There is none like you

Words and Music: Lenny LeBlanc

© Copyright 1991 Integrity's Hosanna! Music. Administered by Kingsway's
Thankyou Music, P.O. Box 75, Eastbourne, East Sussex, BN23 6NW, UK. (For the UK only.) Used by permission.

Acknowledgements

The publishers wish to express their gratitude to the following for permission to include copyright material in this book:

The Anglican Church of Canada, 600 Jarvis Street, Toronto, Ontario M4Y 2J6, Canada for the extract from Rooted in God: *Parables from the Garden* by Marcia Hollis, © 1983 Marcia Hollis. Published by Anglican Book Centre and used by permission.

CopyCare, P.O. Box 77, Hailsham, East Sussex BN27 3EF (music@copy-care.com) for the songs *When I feel the Touch* © 1978 Word's Spirit of Praise Music; *All to Jesus I surrender* © HarperCollins Religious, and *Purify my heart* © 1990 Mercy/Vineyard Publishing.

Hodder and Stoughton Ltd, 338 Euston Road, London NW1 3BH for the extracts from The New International Version of the Bible, © 1973, 1978, 1984 International Bible Society. All rights reserved. (NIV is a registered trademark of International Bible Society. UK trademark number 1448790)

Kingsway Publications, Lottbridge Drove, Eastbourne, East Sussex BN23 6NT, UK for the extract from *The Father Heart of God* by Floyd McClung, 1985.

Kingsway's Thankyou Music, P.O. Box 75, Eastbourne, East Sussex BN23 6NW, UK for the songs *Abba Father, let me be* © 1977; *Overwhelmed by love* © 1994; *God is here, God is present* © 1987; *Father God I wonder* © 1984; *I'm your child* © 1991; *Jesus, take me as I am* © 1978; *There is none like you* © 1991 Integrity's Hosanna! Music; *Only by grace* © 1990 Integrity's Hosanna! Music, and *Give thanks with a grateful heart* © 1978 Integrity's Hosanna! Music.

Make Way Music, P.O. Box 263, Croydon, CR9 5AP, UK for the song *O Father of the fatherless* © 1992. International copyright secured. All rights reserved.

The Reverend Derek Osborne for the extract from *Let the Light Shine* by Derek Osborne, published by Falcon Booklets/CPAS Publications.

Sovereign Lifestyle Music Ltd, P.O. Box 356, Leighton Buzzard, Beds. LU7 8WP, UK for the song *Your mercy flows* © 1987.

Tyndale House Publishers Inc., 351 Executive Drive, Carol Stream, Illinois 60188, USA for the Scriptures taken from The Living Bible, © 1971. All rights reserved.

Word Books Inc., USA for the extract from *Balcony People* by Joyce Landorf, © 1984.

Every effort has been made to trace the owners of copyright material and we hope that no copyright has been infringed. Pardon is sought and apology made if the contrary be the case, and a correction will be made in any reprint of this book.